W9-BBV-049

HIP-HOP HEADLINERS

SNOOP DOGG

Gareth Stevens
Publishing

By Kevin Pearce Shea

Please visit our website, www.garethstevens.com. For a free color catalog of all our high-quality books, call toll free 1-800-542-2595 or fax 1-877-542-2596.

Shea, Kevin Pearce.
Snoop Dogg / Kevin Pearce Shea.
    p. cm. — (Hip-hop headliners)
Includes index.
ISBN 978-1-4339-6622-4 (pbk.)
ISBN 978-1-4339-6623-1 (6-pack)
ISBN 978-1-4339-6620-0 (library binding)
1. Snoop Dogg, 1972—Juvenile literature. 2. Rap musicians—United States—Biography—Juvenile literature. I. Title.
ML3930.S68S54 2012
782.421649092—dc23
[B]
                            2011035920

First Edition

Published in 2012 by
Gareth Stevens Publishing
111 East 14th Street, Suite 349
New York, NY 10003

Designer: Andrea Davison-Bartolotta
Editor: Therese Shea

Photo credits: Cover background Shutterstock.com; cover, p. 1 Dr. Billy Ingram/WireImage/Getty Images; pp. 5, 25 Scott Gries/Getty Images; p. 7 Vince Bucci/Getty Images; p. 9 Frank Micelotta/Getty Images; p. 11 Frazer Harrison/Getty Images; p. 13 Amanda Edwards/Getty Images; p. 15 Tony Barson/WireImage/Getty Images; p. 17 Bryan Bedder/Getty Images; p. 19 Dave Hogan/Getty Images; p. 21 Rob Loud/Getty Images; p. 23 Jason Squires/WireImage/Getty Images; p. 27 Kevin Mazur/WireImage/Getty Images; p. 29 Maury Phillips/WireImage/Getty Images.

Printed in the United States of America

CPSIA compliance information: Batch #CW12GS: For further information contact Gareth Stevens, New York, New York at 1-800-542-2595.

Contents

Hip-Hop King

Snoop Dogg is the most famous rapper in the world. He can be seen in movies and on TV, too. He is even famous for the way he talks!

5

Young Snoop

Calvin Broadus Jr. was born on October 20, 1972. His mother thought he looked a bit like Snoopy, the dog in the comics. She called him "Snoop"!

Snoop grew up in Long Beach, California. He was often in trouble. He got mixed up in drugs. He was in fights, too. Snoop spent time in jail.

Snoop had been rapping since sixth grade. He had a special way of rapping. It was more like talking. Snoop discovered making music kept him out of trouble.

Dr. Dre

Snoop recorded music with his friend Warren G. Warren G's stepbrother was rapper Dr. Dre. Dre heard their music. He wanted to work with Snoop Dogg.

Warren G

Snoop worked on Dr. Dre's first album. This gangster rap album came out in 1992. Two songs were top 10 hits on the hip-hop and pop music charts.

Dr. Dre

Next, Snoop worked on his own album. Dr. Dre worked with him. People could not wait to hear it. Snoop's trouble with the law and his songs with Dre had made him famous.

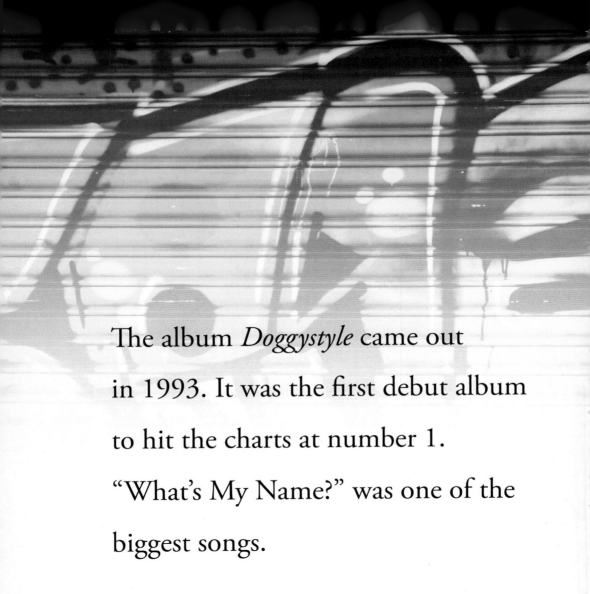

The album *Doggystyle* came out
in 1993. It was the first debut album
to hit the charts at number 1.
"What's My Name?" was one of the
biggest songs.

More Than Music

Snoop's third album was *Tha Doggfather*. It was not a huge hit like his first album. Snoop began to move away from violent gangster rap.

Snoop made many more albums. He began to act in movies and on TV, too. He even wrote a book about his life in 2001! Like his album, it was called *Tha Doggfather*.

Teaming Up

Snoop has worked with many artists. His 2004 song with Pharrell was called "Drop It Like It's Hot." It was his first number 1 song on the hip-hop and pop charts.

Pharrell

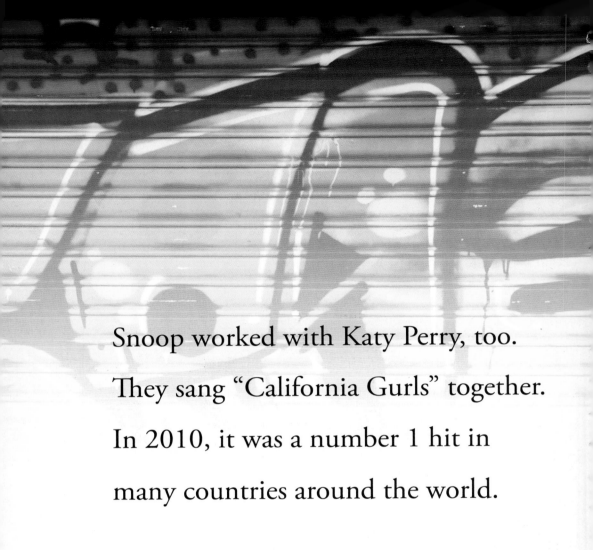

Snoop worked with Katy Perry, too.
They sang "California Gurls" together.
In 2010, it was a number 1 hit in
many countries around the world.

Katy Perry

King Snoop

Snoop still makes music today. In 2011, *The Doggumentary* became his eleventh album. This king of hip-hop will wear his crown for many more years.

Timeline

1972	Calvin Broadus Jr. is born in Long Beach, California.
1992	Dr. Dre's first album has many songs with Snoop.
1993	Snoop's first album comes out.
1996	The album *Tha Doggfather* comes out.
2001	The book *Tha Doggfather* comes out.
2004	"Drop It Like It's Hot" hits number 1 on the charts.
2010	"California Gurls" is another number 1 hit for Snoop.
2011	*The Doggumentary* is Snoop's eleventh album.

For More Information

Books

Carlson-Berne, Emma. *Snoop Dogg*. Broomall, PA: Mason Crest Publishers, 2007.

Earl, C. F. *Dr. Dre*. Philadelphia, PA: Mason Crest Publishers, 2012.

Llanas, Sheila Griffin. *Hip-Hop Stars*. Mankato, MN: Capstone Press, 2010.

Websites

Snoop Dogg
www.mtv.com/music/artist/snoop_dogg/artist.jhtml
Read more about Snoop Dogg's life and albums.

Snoop Dogg
www.billboard.com/#/artist/snoop-dogg/33952
Find new Snoop Dogg songs on the music charts.

Glossary

comics: drawings that are often funny and tell a story

debut: the first time appearing

gangster rap: a kind of rap that tells about violence and life in cities

record: to make a copy of music or sounds

violent: having to do with the use of force to harm someone

Index